PORTABLE KISSES

Tess Gallagher was born in Port Angeles, Washington, the daughter of a logger and longshoreman. A poet, essayist, fiction writer and playwright, she has published many books, including five poetry titles in Britain with Bloodaxe: *My Black Horse: New & Selected Poems* (1995), *Portable Kisses* (1996), *Dear Ghosts,* (2007), *Midnight Lantern: New & Selected Poems* (2012) and *Is, Is Not* (2019). She has published three collections of stories, *The Lover of Horses* (1986), *At the Owl Woman Saloon* (1997) and *The Man from Kinvara: Selected Stories* (2009), plus two books of essays, *A Concert of Tenses: Essays on Poetry* (1986) and *Soul Barnacles: Ten More Years with Ray* (2000). She co-authored two screenplays with Raymond Carver, and later contributed to the making of the Robert Altman film *Short Cuts*, based on Carver's work. She has also written introductions to books such as *A New Path to the Waterfall* and *All of Us* by Raymond Carver and *Carver Country*. She collaborated with the Irish storyteller Josie Gray to set his stories into print in *Barnacle Soup* (Blackstaff, 2007). In 2013 she hosted a Raymond Carver Festival on the Olympic Peninsula where she lived with her late husband until his death in 1988. She spends part of each year in the West of Ireland, near Sligo.

TESS GALLAGHER

Portable Kisses

BLOODAXE BOOKS

ISBN: 978 1 85224 365 4

This edition published 1996 by
Bloodaxe Books Ltd,
Eastburn,
South Park,
Hexham,
Northumberland NE46 1BS
UK

First published in the USA by Capra Press
as *Portable Kisses* (1992)
and as *Portable Kisses Expanded* (1994)

www.bloodaxebooks.com
For further information about Bloodaxe titles
please visit our website and join our mailing list
or write to the above address for a catalogue.

Supported using public funding by
**ARTS COUNCIL
ENGLAND**

Digital reprint of the 1996 Bloodaxe Books edition.

for the breath inside
each kiss

ACKNOWLEDGEMENTS

Four of these poems appeared in a hand-printed limited edition, *Portable Kisses,* from Sea Pen Press & Paper Mill, 2900 21st Ave. South, Seattle, WA in 1978. Still available. The second incarnation of *Portable Kisses* was published by Capra Press in 1992, and acknowledgements are due to the following publications in which poems from that edition first appeared: *The American Voice*: 'Androgynous Kiss', 'Lynx Light' (another version), 'The Kiss Eats a Loaf of Bread', 'The Kiss in Her Bath'; *Colorado Review*: 'Behind Which There Is an Expanse Past the World', 'Black Pearl', 'His Moment', 'Letter to a Kiss That Died for Us'; *Fine Madness*: 'Do I Like It?', 'One Kiss', 'The Destiny Club', 'The Son of Z', 'The Waterfall and the Wolf'; *Hayden's Ferry Review*: 'In the Laboratory of Kisses'; *Michigan Quarterly Review*: 'Fable of a Kiss'; *Ms.*: 'Sugarcane'; *New Letters*: 'Cameo', 'Invaded by Souls', 'Kiss Pressed Like a Flower'; *Ontario Review*: 'Kiss Without a Body', 'Like the Sigh of Women's Hair'; *The Paris Review*: 'Precious'; *Passages North*: 'Widow in Red Shoes', 'Why Do They Talk Sex to Me?'; *Ploughshares*: 'Another Visit from the Love Inspector'; *Poetry Canada Review*: 'Why Do They Talk Sex to Me?', 'Widow in Red Shoes'; *ZYZZYVA*: 'White Kiss'. 'Glimpse Inside An Arrow After Flight' and 'Memory of a Kiss: Fan-Shaped Portrait' (originally 'Fan-Shaped Valentine') appeared in *Louder Than Words: A Second Collection* (Vintage Books, 1991).

'Posthumous Valentine' (first published in *Ploughshares*) and 'Fresh Stain' (first published in *American Poetry Review*) appeared in *Moon Crossing Bridge* (Graywolf Press, 1992), and in *My Black Horse: New & Selected Poems* (Bloodaxe Books, 1995).

An enlarged edition, *Portable Kisses Expanded*, was published by Capra Press in 1994. All the poems in section III were added to this edition, as well as 'Lynx Light' and 'Cameo' in section IV.

The text of this first UK edition of *Portable Kisses* corresponds to that of *Portable Kisses Expanded* (1994). The first part of the introduction appeared as a preface to the 1992 edition, and the second was added to *Portable Kisses Expanded* in 1994.

CONTENTS

INTRODUCTION

1

There are as many nuances and inflections for kisses as there are lips to kiss and moments in which to bestow them.

Why does it seem to me then that poets and teenagers are the protectors and sustainers of the possibilities of kisses? Could it be as simple as the fact that kisses, like words, are dispensed by the mouth? There is, for my own sensibility, the feeling that each word is the embodiment of a synaptic pressure of mind against body.

Kisses, especially as they are written down, seem to carry entire worlds. They are communications beyond and including the sexual. And I've enclosed them within the erotic as it belongs to the I-Thou of love. To sacrament.

As it happens, I began to write these introductory words on the third wedding anniversary of my marriage to Raymond Carver. The *Portable Kisses* of 1978 predates that relationship.

When I think of how the book began, I recall a small fuchsia-colored volume, Pablo Neruda's *Twenty Love Poems and a Song of Despair*, translated by W.S. Merwin. I carried it everywhere in the early 1970s until its cover disintegrated. It was small enough to tuck into my handbag or into the large pockets of my coat. It was something many books of poems are not – portable. I read it in lines at the bank and post office, while waiting for ferry boats, in lecture halls – those times when I got marooned, and needed a little poetry to yank me back to life.

The limited edition printing of *Portable Kisses* turned out to be such a fine production that it wasn't really portable. Nonetheless, the title of the book continued to haunt me, inviting me to attempt some later collection. But this time I wanted a book that could be read in the bath or in an open boat on the Strait of Juan de Fuca when the salmon weren't biting, a book perishable as certain kisses which must be eagerly, even a little recklessly renewed.

When I traveled from Missoula to Dallas, Texas in November of 1977, a book I'd carried with me to the SMU writing conference was Rolfe Humphries' translation of Lorca's *Gypsy Ballads*. I met Raymond Carver there, and in 1979, when we began living together in El Paso, I remember reading aloud to him from this small black book with its red-gilded rose. Lorca's *duende* and the sense of a passionate life were things we both understood, the deadliness of the moment, the beauty inside that, the breaking through of any happiness.

*

Noel Young, a long-time friend and publisher of Ray's, had wanted to print something new of mine ever since Ray and I had published *Dostoevsky: A Screenplay* with Capra in 1985. When I mentioned my often postponed intention to write more 'kiss' poems and offer *Portable Kisses* in paperback, he was delighted.

Most of this book was written during May through September of 1991. I wanted to begin with the wry, sassy tone of the limited edition, then to add a mixture of love poems and poems pointedly reserved for representing kisses. I conceived of the book in mottled tones – the whimsical alongside the passionate, the panoramic with the close-up, and always the intimacy of the vignette, often simply of a man and a woman speaking quietly to each other in a room.

During this time, an odd thing had begun to happen to my taste for reading poetry. I began to balk at the eight to ten page poems in the literary journals. I seemed to need the high voltage, even the off-handedness of the lyric. I wanted something bite-sized – something a medical student might open to recharge the humors on a sleepless night when the patients on the ward had drifted fitfully but miraculously off. Still, stories, always stories claimed me, those told by others and those I lived from the inside like the one in 'Sugarcane', a poem I'd waited twenty-three years to write.

And yes, I was thinking of the lovers – always in a hurry but dreaming over their tasks, impossibly sidelined by thoughts of the beloved. I hadn't forgotten them. They mustn't be allowed to settle for the few words assembled in the dictionary to describe what a kiss might be: 'to salute, greet, smack, osculate, smooch, bundle, spoon or blow a kiss'!

Since kisses are essences as well as actions, they refuse subordination and aren't, as the sex manuals and some anthropologists would have it, merely preludes to the bed. But when, in a writerly way, I start to treat them with too much decorum, I recall reading an anthropologist's account of the Trobriand Islanders. In that part of New Guinea, the lovers 'suck each other's lower lips, and the lips will be bitten till blood comes'.

*

In the Far East to kiss is a secret activity, 'too personal to talk about', according to my Japanese translator, Emiko Kuroda. But in the West kisses belong to the wide realm of general wit, tenderness and play between intimates. They can be dangerous, even searing as when we read translations from the Russian of Marina Tsvetayeva ('A kiss on the head wipes away memory./ I kiss your head.' Tsvetayeva/Elaine Feinstein 1917). Or the haunting kiss of Bella Akhmadulina:

> O my darling, practice
> magic, let your familiar ring
> with its ice-cold kiss
> touch my forehead with healing.

> [1969: *translated by Geoffrey Dutton and Igor Mezhakoff-Koriakin*]

I'm also partial to the powerful psychic avalanches caused by the printed kisses of Anna Akhmatova:

> There's a sacred limit to any closeness,
> Even the passionate fact can't transcend,
> Though in fearful silence lips on lips may press
> And the heart love tears to pieces won't mend.

> [1915: *translated by Lyn Coffin*]

And now I'm back to Neruda, the King of Kisses, who writes them as a garland and a cherishing. He gave them so they charge us from the blood out with energy for love in its between-ness, its reciprocity.

Even so, in 'The Laboratory of Kisses' experiment reigns, and 'acting upon' is also prelude to discovery. Ideally a reader should finish this book then find somebody to kiss.

TESS GALLAGHER
17 June 1991

2

Perhaps every writer dreams of a book that writes itself, a book with characters and pizazz that won't let you go, even when you put down your pen. The nature of *Portable Kisses* in this expanded edition seems to compel me with exactly this fervor. Even now, I can't be sure there won't be still more 'kiss' poems.

No sooner had I published the 1992 edition than more poems with kisses began to insist on arriving. 'The Kiss' as a character had chosen her birth moment in 'The Kiss Joins the CIA'. Now she basks center stage like a fishwife of the heart's raw daring. Freshened by each incarnation, she flaunts a versatile temper mixed with a vinegary, relentless attention span trained on both political and personal calamities. She is wry and rapacious, a Cool-Hand-Luke of chance and savvy, yet tender and yearning, able for the full range of human foibles. Co-existing with her is the gentler, dream-threaded consciousness of poems like 'Harmless' and 'Invaded by Souls'.

These new arrows in my quiver are at once more societal and interior, the tips inlaid with obsidian and mossy jade, their feathers snatched from the underbody of the Night Heron whose voice is described as a 'harsh raucous *kwock*' in flight and who, like 'The Kiss' presents a 'blood red iris' at close range.

TESS GALLAGHER
12 April 1994

I

From so much loving and journeying, books emerge.
And if they don't contain kisses or landscapes,
if they don't contain a man with his hands full,
if they don't contain a woman in every drop,
hunger, desire, anger, roads,
they are no use as a shield or as a bell:
they have no eyes and won't be able to open them...

PABLO NERUDA
FROM *Ars Magnetica*
translated by Alastair Reid

Portable Kisses

They will take you
with them, stuffing
their fat lips
as they gallop, as they
prance soulfully
up to you with veils

on their wrists,
as they swim the Atlantic
and Indian Oceans
in tuxedos rented in Havana.

They are ready to bribe
the guards who search
your empty luggage
by stomping on it.

All the kisses fly out.
What border?
What passport?

Through glass doors
a lively sonatina
begins to play
just for you.

The Kiss of the Voyeur

is made of lingering.
While the kisses of others
tear greedily the pages of the face,
she uncloaks against time, against breath,
against memory. She releases the velvet
behind darkness, shines there
like a green scarf
on a green bough, outside
his window, all undulation
and savoring. Not wanting that
which he has, but that which is his
as he can never give it.
Not to reap fervency. But fervently
as the fir bough in sea-wind
to yearn to him and so to draw outwardly
his roaming, weightless
gusts and shudders.

The Waterfall and the Wolf

Her hair has turned
to water, its separations
carried into hiding.
What could she wear out
besides a life?

The sides of arrows
or ribs broken
across the woodsman's horse
meant dread
of the mountain, the wolf
lingering in the knot of pines.
His heart of straw, his
sheep's clothing meant to fail
and charm in failing
that disguise.

Even the mountain
owes stillness to the sky.
So the ribs are
to the blood, and the heavy flesh
of her side to each caress.
The sound of water
in one place: 'Let me. Let me.'

The wings of the water
ruffling his lips.

Letter to a Kiss That Died for Us

I have been writing your memoir.
It is like leaving the world
and still finding you there
as you received us, shaped us
and instantly became unrepeatable.
I keep thinking I can write a cheek against
you, if not lips. A magnetic cheek
with the taste of cold, metallic air
on it so the clang of it will stay
a little after. I tempt you with nakedness
on a terrace, with tambourines, all my gypsy
favors. With the sleek flanks of longing,
I tempt you who are gone forever,
a thought I can have
as this letter is written
outside any death.

Widow in Red Shoes

A quiet gathering of a few old friends,
my first time with some of them
since his death. Getting ready, I think
of greeting them without him, and know
back of a momentary awkwardness,
there's an unstoppable avalanche
none of us will release. Tsvetayeva was right
in mourning Rilke – to cry is
to accept: '*As long as I don't cry he hasn't
died.*' Then I see them –
the red shoes, thrown into my bag
as afterthought, the spiked exclamation points
of the heels, the sharp toes out of the 60s.
They're a little worn. Not easy to replace,
a pair of shoes which went everywhere with
him. Already they have the look
of something misunderstood. I pull on
the black tights, some sort of low-waisted dress,
and slip on the shoes. He always loved
me in these red shoes. Defiant, sexy
and with him.

His Moment

They burned my bed. Took it high
and burned it, those smoldering angels
so eager to lift my one love from earth.

Now that I sleep on the ground
my bed is everywhere.
Now that I kiss the air
my love goes everywhere.

If his are the only lips,
am I never to be kissed
except as one never-to-be-kissed-again?

Sometimes the dawn sky clings
to itself like that
in the moment just after multitudes of stars
have faded. That's why I love most
the moment when you take your lips away.

Fresh Stain

I don't know now if it was kindness – we do
and we do. But I wanted you with me
that day in the cool raspberry vines, before
I had loved anyone, when another girl and I
saw the owner's son coming to lift away
our heaped flats of berries. His
white shirt outside his jeans so
tempting. That whiteness, that quick side-glance
in our direction. We said nothing,
but quickly gathered all the berries we could, losing
some in our mirth and trampling them
like two black ponies who only want to keep their backs
free, who only want to be shaken with
the black night-in-day murmur of hemlocks
high above. Our slim waists, our buds
of breasts and red stain of raspberries cheapening
our lips. We were sudden, we were
two blurred dancers who didn't need paradise. His shirt,
his white shirt when the pelting ended, as if
we had kissed him until his own blood
opened. So we refused every plea and
were satisfied.

You didn't touch me then, just listened
to the cool silence after. Inside,
the ripe hidden berries as we took up our wicker baskets,
our hands lost past the wrists
in the trellised vines. Just girls with the arms of
their sweaters twisted across their hips, their laughter
high in sunlight and shadow, that girl
you can almost remember as she leans into the vine,
following with pure unanswerable desire, a boy
going into the house to change his shirt.

Posthumous Valentine

You want me to know I'm keeping memories
so you unlatch a few. The future's
in there too, badly restrained
like an actress so intently fastened on
her cue: 'pocketknife' – she stumbles out
on 'doctor's wife' and, mistaken
for the maid, is chased out so as not
to interrupt the kiss. But that's already in
the past. I remember how nicely stingy
they were – streamlining my impromptu
intervals like a serious canoe just
composed enough for two.

Another Visit from the Love Inspector

I'm never home when he knocks his speculum
on my breastbone. It would be fair
to say I've developed an immunity against his
questionings and furtive gougings. Our interviews
are conducted through the keyhole which reduces
him to a button, a hyphen of thread linking two black nostrils.

He is a swashbuckler of swoonable fragments.
I correct his hesitational judgments which leak speechward
into my love nest – his more-than-hints that all love
becomes pathological at the death-instant of
one of the lovers. Such love has 'the moment', he says,

of a baseball game played in 1959. We know the score,
now it's time to play ball. He slaps
his mitt. The ball whizzes past the plate. It has a lot of spin
on it. I call the spin 'the ghost-of-my-home-run-love'.
I muscle up to it. I am going to knock it out of
this park. Out of this pate, this bald pate

with its vigorous agenda, its nostalgia-police and its
baton-twirling display of one of us as 'the deceased'.
Okay. I'll watch the ball this time.
And if I *Babe Ruth* it out of this life, the park will be so big
neither of us will live to record
our jointly implausible, our once-and-for-spacious descent.

Sinister Memory

In your genuine skeleton
you're striding bald and irreversible
up the corridors of expert physicians,
of dentists with long memories, you
with the blue bandana tied
to your neck bones.

Meanwhile I've survived three heart attacks
by breathing inside my mouth.
You say you don't remember the flesh side
of your bones. Also the loving's better
when you don't look
into anyone's eyes. Otherwise
a trumpet goes off in your face or
in the other face or both faces at once.
Silly things get said like, 'Did you hear
that trumpet?' One of you will end up
lying to keep the other company. Already
you're making that false move, kissing me
before I can stop you.

A hummingbird has mistaken me for an open window.
Each feather starts to fly. The bird
takes the point of view of a bird
with our eyes inside, crisscrossing the body
like kisses which just miss.
Inside ourselves we hear humming.

It's final.
We won't get out of this one.

Lucid Valentine

I loved him like a soldier – at the ready,
at full alert. I did not guess our enemy,
a season wide and soft as dawn.
And if my smile when he looked back
seemed to stay like daylight as a moon
would know it – the slow shock of too many
presences – such smiles can wear a world
away, or linger like kisses in February, or
a wreath of birds to crown black hair
on a day full of animal sheen, its coldest rifle
pressed to the heart until we echo and go.

Precious

He gave me a spruce lap desk
for writing in bed that Christmas.
Rubbed into fragrance with oil of almond,
so to lift the slanted top was to fall
into reveries with pens and the child's delight
in things unused. But it lay heavily
against my knees, as if a lid had closed
on me. It saddened him, I know, to see
how seldom I used it. Some gifts are sent
only to haunt. How lightly it rests
the length of my thighs, and lightly my pen
against the page under its downcast lids.

II

Love, what a long way, to arrive at a kiss —

PABLO NERUDA

Stubborn Kisses

This kiss won't ride in a car
even with you
in the back seat looking dangerous
as mink. It insists
on running alongside the window
like a piece of the scenery
that won't give you up.

See that splatter, right
where you thought for a moment
it was beautiful? Insects
die over and over
just to prove the sky
is lived-in like this heart
for which I have been given
an inferior sign.

Soon you'll get tired, worrying
about the car running over
my feet, worrying
for the child in me
that's attracting
all these mothers
like a bad parade. You'll
tell the driver to stop
and let you out.

I'll let you
out. I'll stop
and let you out.

Fable of a Kiss

I was lonely. Very shortly
I was lonely again.
I found myself in my mother's orchard
but she was nowhere about.
I pulled a plum
from her plum tree and took a bite.
It was bitter, mixed with
a puzzling unripeness of my own
that made me feel I had lost everything.

Birds came and went from the trees.
A brown snake slid into the iris bed.
I took a vicious bite
from the plum. It seemed to know
it had befallen my hard jaw
and participated in its violent addition.
My mouth ached: the plum flesh
shoved itself along in me
down to the shaggy pit
where loneliness changes to solitude,
and what was bitter slips
into another register, a woman's
footsteps, her kiss
on the forehead,
which for the mother
is another mouth.

Even if she is missing,
perhaps long dead, the story
of her one-time child
under a plum tree
is a kind of snare to press the lips
of the mind against, an inexact
comfort that is also a pang
and a forfeit
as the ceremony of the ever-unloved heart
unfolds, contracts, unfolds.

Why Do They Talk Sex to Me?

The men are always young and virile, hurrying
to keep up with demand – one, a poet,
told me he hardly had time to rush home, shower and
change underwear before his next
assignation. The fire in my grate
crackles and leaps, then dies down when
they leave, jauntily magnetized to
the next opportunity.

Or the one at the jazz bar drumming his palms against
the table, who describes an afternoon
at a certain inn near a lake. 'That lake's
beautiful from the upstairs rooms,' I say, remembering
so the voice carries its silence. 'I didn't
notice,' he says. 'Too busy making
love.' My eyebrow quivers, he
looks down, then up
a little shyly. 'Well, maybe not love, then.'
'No, maybe not,' I say, and smile tenderly as if he were
only a boy with things to learn. But he's nearly
fifty, lightly anchored to
a girl of twenty-seven who lives
in another state and who subsists on phone calls and
an occasional long weekend.

Then there was the story of that one's wife, getting
older, and how he'd encouraged her to have
a few drinks – the sex better, but she was
drunk, right? what kind of situation
is that? he said, and ate a handful of crackers from
the plate, washed down with Polish vodka.

I'm like a cedar tree the bees moved stickily
about inside before it was robbed
by berry pickers or bears. Even so,
its trace of lost sweetness
reminds them disarmingly of something they wanted once,

something that could be taken away entirely and not
replenished – not these half loves, these
bad songs on convenient jukeboxes. But sure,
here's a quarter. Here's two. The nights are long.
Yes, I'm listening. See what you can find.

Poems Written About Kisses

Many real things like darkness falling
to the emptied playground or to a ship's flag
happen outside anticipation or afterthought.
But kisses on their way to us
are easily becalmed
or, once accomplished, turn back
so quickly to where they came from
we scarcely breathe out
and they are fictive
as rain which fell yesterday.
So if I write: 'my lips are still wet with kisses,'
it is like photographs of fire,
the avaricious portraiture
of actions sealed imperfectly
by the gleam of memory. We must add heat
and the fear that someone may not
have gotten out alive. Consider
then the half-closed eyes
of love's pensive listening to old rain
in the mind's greedy vault. Rain
I used to know, falling onto this page
as rain yet to fall – lightly, lightly –
though kisses are torrent and torment
yesterday or tomorrow, and a poem,
like anything propelled by absent power,
eats and drinks nothing, sustains
as it consumes.

The Destiny Club

I spot it like you snap an ace down
on formica. 'Pull over,'
I tell my friend. We've just eaten
pancakes with gravy on the side.
Life is rich but the future
could tumble. We walk in
feeling Texan, ready for anything,
and sit down at the bar
in the beery shoe-dark of the place.

Back in the corner two lovers
are kissing like wrestlers, a disguise
thrown up to make us think this is
some ordinary dive. 'We've been
expecting you,' a voice says,
back in the gloom. The air
is prehensile, like the modulated hysteria
of fish tanks at seafood restaurants.

The light around my hands has an aqua
wakefulness. 'This is it?' my friend asks.
'All the way for this?' Luckily
there's friction from those two in the corner.
The place bursts into flame and we beat it
with our eyebrows singed. Initiations
are like that, devoted to opposing
parables, escape or endurance,
each decorative evasion irresistible
as new love confirmed at the tomb
of the doomed lovers.

Do I Like It?

One man in my kitchen,
another on the phone, surely
I should have gotten beyond
this. When are you leaving?
I say to one. When are you
coming? to the other. He's
mousing and can't be
discouraged. All day he arranges
his approach: Was so and so
your lover? then reading
my poems aloud in his
sweet round accent, pausing
to dab violet at the heart
of the pansy. I'm watching
shore birds, how away from water
they prefer to land in the unsteady
tops of trees. When we finally kiss
I say, 'Give me your tallest.
Let it be a long way
down from here.'

Kissing the Blindman

is like kissing the moon
between phases, a kind of larceny
that sweetens one light as it
quenches another. He was halls
and handsomely, a drowned lamp
in my skull, a ship in the mountain,
silk over no shoulder.

Black moon before breath,
I don't kiss you with my mouth only,
but like an ivory hand reaching for dice
thrown across marble.
We roll and roll into the echo's
last chamber.

Androgynous Kiss

It is not the sex washed out
but intensified past its difference –
the archangel Saint Michael painted
by Gentile da Fabriano with his wings
crossed to shelter his too omnipotent sex.
Or Joan of Arc in armor stroked
in a scald of black against red velvet
by Rubens, her burnished hair
flowing, the iron gloves laid by,
her hands bare, praying.

Where is that point of intersection
between holy and unholy? they asked of her
who was never unaccompanied
because she believed in her voices, even
when they changed her story: Margaret
of Antioch in holy simplicity tending sheep
as the Roman prefect sullenly rides by;
Saint Catherine of Alexandria, patron saint
of prisoners, tortured on the wheel, tended
then by angels.

Still the Maid's accounts were restrained,
unadorned by supernatural
ornament. Always to accept the miracle
but to refuse adoration. Kiss of
sacrament, kiss of private fervor,
friendless kiss of the virgin pledged
to God alone. Rarest kiss of innermost blood
and the arrow six inches deep between her neck
and shoulder. Under her, the duke's black horse,
deemed holy as her sword
which, as she said, 'gave good blows
and good slashes'.

One Kiss

A man was given one kiss, one
mouth, one tongue, one early dawn, one boat
on the sea, lust of an indeterminate
amount under stars. He was happy
and well fitted for life until he met a man
with two cocks. Then a sense of futility
and of the great unfairness of life befell him.
He lay about all day like a teenaged girl dreaming,
practicing all the ways to be unconsciously beautiful.

Gradually his competitive spirit began to fade
and in its place a gigantic kiss rowed toward him.
It seemed to recognize him, to have intended itself
only for him. It's just a kiss, he thought,
I'll use it up. The kiss had the same thing
on its mind – 'I'll use up this man.'

But when two kisses kiss, it's like tigers
answering questions about infinity with their teeth.
Even if you are eaten, it's okay – you just become impossible
a new way – sleepless, stranger than fish, stranger
than some goofy man with two cocks. That's
what I meant about the hazards
of infinity. When you at last begin to seize those things
which don't exist,
how much longer will the night need to be?

Memory of a Kiss: Fan-Shaped Portrait

What was blue is lavender now, as wishfulness
accordions the paleness from a morning
in a furl of heartbeats – what those
gulls may feel, flying through a rain-
bow seen to be raining. Our twin
silences thicken us with shafts
of pouring light. Good always
to keep slatted sandalwood to
arc below the eyes in a
flush of air, the more
to bare an arched
wrist, the naked
back of hand.

The Kiss Joins the CIA

When she received her first assignment
they gave her three aliases
and one pseudonym. For a while
she kept mixing herself up
like a multidirectional homonym.
They gave her a kit with purple
lipstick, a goatee, a blond wig and falsies.
Evidently her predecessor
had been multipurpose, but he'd bought it
in Belgrade when some Chetnik, savoring orders,
straddled him in a doorway.

'How about something practical, like
a little chapstick?' she quipped
to her operations officer.
They strapped the latest in miniature
artillery above her ear, a revolver
the size of a cricket. Instead of
a trench coat they instructed her
in the art of the kimono. Her obi
wrapped around her four times.
It had been handed down
for generations like a samurai sword,
last worn by a male agent
who'd performed kabuki.
Never mind the bloodstains
on the exaggeratedly billowing sleeves.

But how could she work in such
a getup? Just so, she was told, she wasn't
to initiate. Her contacts
would come to her. No more poisoned
capsules either. Wart-sized Band-Aids
were affixed to her teeth. 'And use this
at all times,' her boss said, handing her
a see-through prophylactic fan.

When they gave her the operation code
written in lemon juice she waited
until she was in the alley to strike
a match. It read: *Kiss of Death.*
She smiled a purple smile.
Nothing like starting at the top.

Generic Kiss

Like a daybreak moon it misses
its lantern, but reconciles
by fading into each translucent
face. If you receive one
it will cost less than devotion.
Give it and it will stay put
unemphatically like a hedge
around a turnstile. We inhabit
them for leave-takings
which overlap arrivals, a kind of
doorless hinge that swings
by fictitious mutuality.
For meeting those we used
to love in the company of those
we do, they serve well as camouflage,
to blot the ambiguous residue
of invitation. They can be bold
like a white chair on a green lawn
at dusk, or hushed as lilac dedicated
to allure because no one
claimed pleasure. Still it was there
as attitude, that intention to lift
the pulse, yet keep repose.
'I suppose,' she said,
and vanished.

Let Me Kiss Also the Ground

When I met the Major General
he inquired, 'Have you kisses for all else
and none for the ground?'
Take me, I said, to Balaclava
where eighteen hundred chargers
fell. Someone should walk that ground
with a memory of those deaths
in their unchosen war. Let me kiss also
the ground where in three years
three hundred thousand British cavalry mounts
went down. A horse dead
for every three miles travelled.
There should be an angel assigned to bless
those sacrificed spirits, Major General.
But, falling far short of an angel, I'll go.
In memory, I will go there, first
to Balaclava.

The Son of Z

When he steps ashore
with the air of a smuggler
I profess the bowl of my spoon,
the trance of my spoon, the mastery
of my busy spoon, when he steps ashore.
For he is the son of Z, ornamentation
to an ending, all there is of vessel
and voyage and sea. His cargo
is kisses and candles.
My cache of spoons recalls
those missing from this island.

No matches to be had
for the candles, sir. But any kiss
finds its complement. Two by two
I light them, Mister Z, daylight
or dark, mutinous company, Mister Z.

III

for the eyes of the deer
for the eyes of the cougar
the kiss

The Kiss Takes Confession

He was a man between two women,
that condition of amplitude guaranteed
to overvalue. He basked quietly
in their desperate spillover
meant to hold him. With honesty
as policy he'd kept each informed
about the other, as if honesty could
convert duplicity to some well-meaning
by-product of his foamy
approximation at consideration.
He glimpsed in himself the pride
of 'character' which he recirculated
between them as sauce to himself,
an accolade meant to disarm
their chief suspicion, that he would
have it all, and scant of guilt.

The Kiss, like a devouring beauty,
perched on his knee as he turned
the pages of his scrapbook. There
stood his young wife, glowing like a lily,
translucent in the blue frieze
of time, next to their child. She
does not know fate will comb
her skull with ashes. How radiantly
she wears the waxy glow of the candle
assaulted by its flame!
She was never, he confessed with a sigh,
his soul mate, though the years had 'coded
her into' his DNA – which explained
this guest house he ran between them.

The other woman, he warned, would soon
step through the doorway. The Kiss
drew herself to attention, and, not to be blinded
by barbarous light, slipped on her sunglasses.
Trembling and pursing her lips
she stared toward the entry.

A knock came. The man's face, resplendent
with welcome, veered round the room
like a drunken swallow. The likeness
of his soul stepped toward them,
wizened as a prune, this crone
whose tactile longings had the pizazz
of beauty and had brought him to his powers.

The Kiss racked her shades, the better
to admire their mutual palpitations, this dream-love,
an emanation from the back of his mind
where the covenant of his unhappiness
was at last complete. Truly now, something
had to give. And it wasn't her.
And it wasn't him.

Wimp Love

is good at desire, but unsustainable
as the most ferocious bonfire.
You have to die down with it
before nightfall, to be willing
to consign yourself to a hiatus of
roseate ashes. Like anything unsure
of its worth, it glamorizes itself by
scorching whatever it touches
with passionate invitation, then
as it falls into a love-sick coma, flashes
its Amnesiac Diploma.

The Kiss in Her Bath

She took her water lobster-pot steaming,
was of the scorch and soak school, lowered herself
in – feet, then fanny first – cursed
a little, adjusted her haunches, leaned deeply
into herself like a gambler hunched
to a Royal Flush or a firewalker easing onto glowing coals,
throwing off sparks of sadness and joy, a sizzling
abundance hot-footing it to some other side of just-made-it
imperviousness. Her imperial mock-daring
was haughty as the bloody lip-prints
she'd squandered once in Paris against Napoleon's tomb.
She adored the taste, the waste
of marble. The horrified guard caught a glimpse
of her like a huge, wicked insect chilling herself
with a final history-melting, corpse-hailing kiss-cry
as she soared crisply onto the sill, having added
her rude commentary to history's redolent self-love.

She shut her eyes.
Splashed a few vials of holywater across
her breasts, leaned back into the chin-high bubbles.
The day had wearied her. She'd been kissing babies
for politicians all afternoon. The smell of talc had
made her nauseous and she detested all those googoo-eyed,
plum-cheeked excursions into the flesh and blood future.
She freshened her suds with scalding water
at the tap, reached for a cigar, lit it
from a candle at her elbow – the reek of chubby,
blear-eyed promise receding
with each global puff. Still, one bambi-throated toddler
had clamped to her mouth with such fervor
she couldn't disengage. Her face was a violet pucker
before her bodyguard seized, then yanked the bumpkin off. What
suction! Who would he or she
turn out to be? The Kiss mused, blew a few votive heart-shapes
imagining – Helen of Troy, Mozart, Billie

Holliday, Dizzy Gillespie. The more her bubbles
sank, the more she soared. She was red-hot, this momma, never
to be forgotten by those diaper-rashed tribes
she'd inspired as their first misbegotten orgy – pleasure
with a stranger. She felt a twinge
of compunction, but sponged free figuring she'd be subliminal,
an inexplicable, embryonic craving for French perfume, blue skies,
kisses tart as winter apples, the thatched stench
of cigars. The fresh turf of babies struck her
with double-fisted fury. She applied a little pumice
to a knee. Felt unashamedly
a not unpleasant subterranean streaming. Great-bladdered
in the luke warm bath, she raised the temperature
one salty degree.

The Kiss Eats a Loaf of Bread

She startled awake, looked around her.
All night kissing icons and new-borns – cold-hot,
cold-hot, silence, then screaming. She was glad
to hobble back to the real world
for some respite.

On the counter sat a loaf of bread.
The white, cottony bread of childhood.
The Kiss, a little miffed at there being
no one around to kiss, applied the reddest
lipstick she could find, hoping to attract
something kissable, the way her mother
used to powder her face white to invoke
an errant island of red invitation
for the trip to the supermarket.

It was a longish day. She'd had to reapply
lipstick several times to keep her hopes
up. She snapped the glossy pages of a magazine
on the coffee table, seeking a little
titilation. Sure enough, it opened
to a photograph of a matador in skintight
swimming trunks. Even though it was
black and white, she knew the gouges
in his thighs meant he'd risked his
life, been gored by bulls, suffered
miscalculations, narrow escapes – the braille
of lives lived outside mere living.

The text said the matador had been 'swung
on the horns' before being 'flung to
the ground'. There had been 'several trajectories
from the main wound'. But since he'd healed
nicely, none of this mattered. Penicillin
had been discovered. He'd lived to display
himself in this provocative pose. She
bent her lips to the page and began to kiss

the white gashes while he stood
transfixed by her eyebrows.

The kisses welling up in her were faintly
pornographic, but when she noted the date
under the photo, she saw her matador
had been dead for years. Still, he made
a beautiful corpse. And who could blame her
for breathing life back into him for that moment?
He was still perpendicular, still
faintly smiling into the afternoon sunlight.

But what's left once you've kissed
a dead matador? Raw whispers from the wounds
of his many near-deaths clung to her mouth.
It was then she sought out
the white bread, took in slice after slice,
leaving rakish, red destinies
before her with every voracious bite.

'Don't spare me!' she cried to the dwindling loaf.
When it was gone she felt refreshed,
a little smug. Never again would she
underestimate the power of white bread
or the resurrections of matadors.

The Kiss Gets a New Bonnet

Shadowed gaze
        of a woman
jolting west on the back
of a buckboard, her face, its

fearful
      inner room,
its face-cave
recessed to the far wall.

What it must have been
to lean into
        the cloistered astrology
of her day-swallowed moment
under fields of insomniac stars!

Did any
      diamond-drop a kiss,
pearl buttons stairstepped
to her ankles, teeth-clicking
        the white eyes of sleep
down to those high-laced boots?
Now *that* – my eyelash, my black sash –

would have been living! and what to do
but cry
      'surround me, night!'
Or to let her
       spill herself like a fun house mirror,
silk butterfly coaxing underneath
of chin, that ivory
        shelf upturning its
sudden cat to her soft-shouldered
hissing, more kissing than could

mire a wagon
        though it upended
wheat fields of swallows whose
heartswoop lifted skyward
my bonnet, my bayonet,
           my lustrous
plush. How she could
         arabesque
a knapsack into
        can't-wait lilt
and plea! Just she, lusty and laughing
in her bonnet at the bottom of some

so-blue
        anything-but-mystery.
No hindsight.
No history. Scarcely a murmur.
Night and moon.

Little Invitation in a Hushed Voice

Even birds help
each other. Come
close. Closer.
Help me
      kiss you.

Kiss Pressed Like a Flower

It was the only faithful kiss
misfortune had put in her way.
Still it kept flying out at her
then going flat, the way lips
have to, inwardly,
waywardly unseeking. A kiss
like someone laying claim in a too loud voice
to the pure and sacred
which dooms as it lasts – especially
when love has been squeezed out of us
and life no longer
insists: 'Here is a surprise for you!'

Like all pressed things, its message
protracts by insinuating
that what has been saved can be
reborn in us by time's very attempt
to separate us from that 'once'
in which we stretched our necks so
tenderly towards each other
it was a blazing up of some black
brilliant creature. Soon
there is nothing to do but flutter and close.
Like the slow eyelid of a wound – or
someone followed ridiculously
from a room by a sofa
having stood up in the 'for certain'
of making up your mind
to live without him. And then.
You did.

Motoring Toward Seattle
The Kiss Considers Capital Punishment

The radio talk-host cheeps sexless
as a neutered chickadee
between the women – both
have lost daughters, the details grizzly – fingers
hacked from a hand, stab wounds punctilious
as a pickaxe for hire, a mire of entrails,
the throat – a duffle bag of blood
unzipping – followed by lively rape performed
by the murderer to a corpse's twitch
and pitch. No wonder the host careens
like a choirboy ratcheting octaves.

One woman, her voice alabaster
with the calisthenics of the soul,
has forgiven her daughter's killer, and
with equanimity, both practical and wise,
advises clarity of heart and rehabilatory zeal
instead of sizzling the mucker
who stole for ransom her seven-year-old
from a tent, then slashed her up
and down with horror until she went
lamb-like into the sweet forever.

Her reconciliation with the slayer evolved,
this mother said, in the raw chambers
of her heart, where God, as witness, shelters
all, even that unholy blin
at the fringe of the human galaxy
she'd wanted barehandedly, at first, to strangle.

The other woman reads from a tract
unpronounceable proclamations on justice,
her voice laced with unabsolvable pain.
She'd been 'made use of by a bloodthirsty State',
suggested the gentled woman, cleansed
of hate. Why trade her mother's soul in revenge
to score victory on the already damned?

What death could retrieve or pay for
that woman's purloined daughter or her own
seven-year-old? And wasn't it mockery to think
that frying that piece of stink before he'd a chance
at remorse was anything but bad ecology?
For what was flesh and blood but the Silly Putty
of the soul, traded out like pork barrels
on God's unfathomable exchange.

Yet kindness held no sway with that mother
whose heart clamped certain value
to a face. She lamented the ease with which
the murderer, convicted and strapped to the chair,
transcending life, blazed past her icy stare,
then slumped like a bag of victuals for eager worms.

The Kiss heard them out like the Archangel
of the Miraculous Ear, fathomed at last
that involuntary invention entrusted most
poignantly to women – the tear. She gripped
the wheel and splashed her way through torrents.
'Kill the bastards with kindness!' she shouted
when she reached the ferry, then fell
upon the boatman with an oarlock.

Harmless

It was nothing, she told him, less
than nothing. Just a kiss attached
to a tunnel, attached
to nights and days of tunneling.
There wasn't a glimmer
of light in that kiss. It passed
through and under. It journeyed on
and on like a dream without anyone dreaming it.
There was no one to wake up and shake
the daylight into things again.

But after enough time had unraveled,
time itself became pure expectation,
a black waterfall with a kiss flourishing
sleek and lovely in its all over, cascading blackness.
It was a vertigo of blackness out of which
the tunnel fed on and on
into the inexplicable recesses of that moment
in which the kiss had somehow begun.

During all this time, a long white beard
had grown around the kiss. But the word 'white'
only occurred like the ghost of a firefly
in one of their minds or in the mind of
the tunnel. Maybe the beard was ebony
as her teeth pressing the tunnel into his cranium
within which, as they discovered, a perfectly matching
tunnel had always existed, and was now linked
to hers. Where were they tunneling to?

Long ago a kiss. Forever more a kiss, tunneling through
roots and cooling aquifers, through cores of molten heat,
through lost mountains and skies-in-the-making.
A solitary kiss like the shaft of an arrow without
an arrowhead, nonetheless able to pierce the farthest side
of this earthly, inhuman globe. A kiss traveling
so intently it arrives in the great spaces between the stars

like an immense, freshly extinguished single eye –
blackly looking, blackly satisfied
with apparitions of light here and there,
battalions of sparks shot out of its own progress
down the interminable, implosive body
of its kissing.

Invaded by Souls

*'... but I'm always being invaded by others' souls
so I can't see my own soul very well.'*

SHUNTARO TANIKAWA

One night you fall asleep with an ungiven kiss
on your lips, you fall asleep in your kiss.
It is like sending yourself on an all night errand
to interview echoes about where they think
they're coming from. Where did it come from
anyway, your falling-asleep kiss? your
good-for-eternity soul?
How do you know they aren't imposters,
your unclouded kiss, your sublimated-soul?

To kiss and return a kiss is to be invaded
by souls, like a dead artist or a living poet,
like the twin sails of a ship in its sky-filled
sex act with the wind. Sometimes
we are taken charge of by the freedom of all those stones
children threw at nothing into the sky or into
the ocean from the Stone Age onward. We are
invaded by souls. We can't hold ourselves back
from each other then.

And besides, you've fallen asleep in your kiss.
Suddenly you are in a railway station
in a state of undress, naked except for your kiss
which, like your soul, is invisible and ungiven.
A whistle blows like a missed rendezvous with
the rest of your life. Souls are rushing past and into
you out of the vast Everything.
There is a dark frame around this absence
called 'the dream'. You are trying to exit
the wrong way down a stairwell invaded by souls.

You'd like to kiss your way out of this like a gangster
of the Starry Moment, but there are too many of them,
these lonely, imperishable souls rushing at you
full of desire and paradox, with wide pockets
of illumination and, as if to prove this is an American
dream and these are American souls,
some are riddled with bullets, cosmetically
punctuated with a certain brutal frankness.

But our capacity for love belongs to the birdsong
of antiquity which cleanses our dream-eyes and
allows them to mix moonlight with starlight
in those phosphorescent kisses multitudes
of plankton give the night.
They kiss with their whole beings, invisibly
sucking the fingertips of the dream's halflife.
Your own soul is in there too
filling up its tank on Infinite Joy and Diversity.
I don't know what else to tell you, except
you'll know when it happens.
A certain restless undulation as with waves
under fog. It's the souls, moving in.

IV

A paper bird I have in my chest...
To live! To live! No one sees the sun crackle,
kisses or birds, late or on time or never.

VICENTE ALEIXANDRE
FROM *Life*
translated by Robert Bly

Glimpse Inside an Arrow After Flight

Two arrows glanced off each other
flying in the same direction, both
still falling, though I have charge of the memory
that one struck the ground – as if memory
could retrieve it. But once on earth
we have the privilege of staying – for only then
are we able to outdistance
every living need
in something like a death. To seem
unpresent in our most ongoing
presence. How else could it happen
that I will never live long enough
to reach the other side
of this memory without you?

Name shouted down a well, name
of someone known and loved, name I say
in perfect faith I won't be answered – keep
your silence. If you spoke back
these things we have yet to mean
would have finished, would have
left us behind
as the past of a word in air.

In the Laboratory of Kisses

We held our rows of lips
so far outside ourselves
a moon watching
would have known how to
unbewitch itself in water.

Gradually to shed, to be
cold silver to what might
come. And somewhere the chill
of glass on glass, the beakers
being stirred with icicles,
whir of hummingbird to add
suspension, and his lips
so freshly long ago
against my eyelids
I hear the lifting and
the setting down of hooves
just breaking the snow-crust.

Gentle in my black – your mare
will startle. Gentle, the noose
he makes of my glass bead necklace
looped suddenly to draw us
closer still.

Lynx Light

The quilt has slipped
my shoulders. And when
you kiss the knots
in my fate like that
it's as if a lynx
co-exists with a housecat.

Give me winter for constancy
and looking back: most silent because
most decided.

Teach me how to shed
this cold devotion
by which memory
is exchanged for alertness.

Come and go with me – sickle,
black tail lashing this
                    transparent net of birdsong.

That Peculiar Open-Air Feeling
When You Speak to a Painter

I send him away but he doesn't go
away, though he goes.
Someone before me has taught his heart
how to use the tamed sweetness
of being apart. He tells me her stolen
mornings until a cold, incalculable zero
brushes my inner thigh.

Why do I want his kisses more when he didn't
choose her, didn't leave
everything to bridge those worldless
mornings? Is he, even now, carrying my twilights
away in mind of her, to pacify some after-longing,
thinking like a day laborer to save up
the jagged points of our unequal tearing
at the fringe of each letting go?

In the small jar he mixes all the darkest colors,
as if to demonstrate, even in this, how impulse
must claim a little of everything
to get that voluminous blue-gray with its streaks
of red showing through glass, a gift
from her vanished fire
he cannot quite
subdue. Or, does he sense the pull of danger
in this already bereft house nearly inside
the sea – that love,
when it is neither shrine nor scar,
refuses to form itself
as anything less than endless

Notes from the Map of Uncharted Occurrences

One woman in his arms, he proposes a second.
'Hadn't she fantasies to live out?' She thought
a long thought back to the sixties. Had the generation
lived her out of fantasy? And, if a man be judged
by his fantasies, wasn't this pretty stock? One for
the mouth, one for the cock or some such congenial
apportionment of openings? Or did he want to watch,
then come in like applause? Did men always assume
women natural lovers to other women – after all, she'd
be choosing, he said, as if her comfort were most
in mind. She bloodhounded out into her band of

women friends for one to inveigle, a woman
she'd felt tender towards in an airport and held to
past a pertinent send-off kiss. Hadn't the woman confessed –
one night when snow was falling so their talk
seemed the body of some scattered, humbled world – that
she'd experienced such a triad. 'Big deal,' wasn't that what
she'd said? Yet why hadn't she asked for details, who
did what and how and to whom? Where was her curiosity?
She'd let the chance slip and trotted back now as to a cache,
her friend as conscript.

Distantly she heard him in the shower. Distantly saw
herself as if laid out on a table. Odd look
he gave her when she moved a delicate foot, rose to
her elbow and motioned him near with words
to untouch him into her own asking – that he bring the man to her
he could love and give in loving. He was silent then. Not
silent, but pensive like someone come in
from having licked clean the face of a rotted thing
under stars. Then they knew the tongue as the center of
what they shadow-kissed, each into the other, uncontained
in that darkest corner of the night. But did the man
think newly of the man? Had loving, as proposition, stretched
the sinews of his royal 'we' past the outskirts of

wearied fictions until they lay common again,
more true in the delirium of their strange double
murmuring? It was another pair who said in unison, with the
imagined all of them: 'Take me then. I'm yours.'

Palette

'My painting is my palette'
ALFREDO ARREGUIN

He liked to lie felicitously notched,
both of them still in their jeans, crotch to crotch
like prepubescent teenagers, as if the world had a center
they could strike themselves against, nuzzling in, every now
and then at the roseate pit – those long afternoons
of mostly talk, punctuated by the muslin braille of sex
grazing them. 'I'll tell you a story,' he'd say, then float the raft
of his body back to childhood which, because his voice

came from above her, had an angelic, upward heft,
this boy stealing oranges and avocados to hide
in the ground for later, or to eat in secret all at once
with his friends. Always stealing, always pleasure
ambushed, as if choosing wished a violence
on him, as now when a certain sickness of speed from
the past, of hunger as wakefulness, overtook him,
haloed, hallowed him for her. Even when their kisses
unexpectedly came to what was no longer air but respite,
they met at some insisted upon peak of willed

confusion. Their mixing, so dependent on its glazing, its shining
through from underneath, assigns his yellow-into-green
another blue than her green-into-yellow. 'Tell me
a love story,' he says, and she knows it will fail him the way
vitality is a blushing between
forms that, once they are too sustained fall dull as paving stones.
'First,' she says, 'they are vagabonds for life. Life jumps
back from them at the slightest contact.' She means its
butterfly-aliveness, more resonant for those intermittent lapses
into retrograde caterpillar winglessness. His mouth

in the crook of her neck appeals, 'No. No. Not like that.
More – a little more beauty.' But like his childhood stealing,
too much beauty makes her queasy. 'Okay,' she says, 'he

thinks of her as a black butterfly with a red rose
imbedded in her forehead.' He has a way now, takes
over from her: '*Con besos delicados* he dusts the black powder
of mourning from her wings, her words full of color and
arrows.' She begins to feel it then, a blue so bright
his Spanish plays suddenly over them: *del amor*

que reparte coronas de alegría. Why then
are their heads bare? But the question is a beseeching,
a blue-black fanning that wafts the marrow
in little breaths to fall back
from, as patience on its transformative way maintains its
fluctuations of distress – a passion
that glooms the soul, great and dark, great and dark.

'del amor/ que reparte coronas de alegria': of love which
distributes crowns of joy – FEDERICO GARCÍA LORCA

Anatomy of a Kiss

This impersonation of an unbitten apple, how
can it add to itself when it is so unformed
by desire that its three mouths skim
the torso and lift away
like the hands of a child brushing
the cool keys of a piano
as she runs through a house
in summer? He runs through her
house in summer. In the garden the kiss
is effacing itself
with a contrary obedience.
It wants to evolve by driving itself
away from him. The child
passes through the house again
and pulls its fist down the keyboard.
From outside the house the rivulet of sound
is a gulp of brandy after which
the eyes close and a voice calls softly
like someone entering a house
where the doors are left open
in summer near dusk. Time
for the child to come in, but it wants to
sleep under trees. Time for the kiss
to speak the bewildered name of love
as a flower might drift out to sea.

No, the house is empty and the child
won't come in. The kiss is evolving
its blue tide, is unexplored yet buoyant.
A white sash of piano notes pulls across
the night sky. The child
curls itself around the sleep it is making
under trees. It is summer
and the doors of the house are open
as the kiss is open in the unbitten apple.
Love, this is our night sky with its sleeping child
and its buoyant white sash.
Lift your deep hands
to the keyboard.

Behind Which There Is an Expanse Past the World

When it's time to come into her
she says he always turns the light on
because he likes to look at her. Not at, but into.
At the eyes. As if the receiving he wanted
needed to reach beyond the geometry of pursuit, to use
the mind's fixative to close it in, or to be
sure of its sending. But also, she said, she felt it
was his way of actually going further into space
at all points of the body. Because he knew, of course,
that other men didn't have to be most bright so soon.
His gaze was steeple-shaped,

like an embodied triangle, moving out from the eyes
to where he joined her as apex, and into which
both lovers, and lovers before them, had
possibly disappeared, never to be retrieved. Except
once in a while as a child, or as the wish
for a child, the lovemaking carried past volition
into an extension of the triangle's
inner space. And future times into which
the lovers do, in fact, disappear, and leave the triangle
altogether behind, as in that moment when space
reviews its options and means what it's brought
together, the way a rainbow wants to pass

attention on to the imagined, yet unattainable,
treasure, even as its color is avoidance of attention
elsewhere. If the man were making love to
a rainbow he would have to look at it, and
yes, he might. But I am looking with
her man into myself as that lover. That's
the way the triangle is. Suddenly
you're inside. And so is
the world.

Some Bandit Love

He is careless with the joy,
throwing it up in the air like a child you intend
to catch at the last moment near the cliff edge
in order to place the right breath of fear
into its unfeathered heart so it can extend
itself later on. What I would have saved
by grace and intervention, he means to lose
until the second after what seemed
irretrievable. He grows a six-day beard
then shaves it off, scrapes the black stubble
into the river. He holds the reins
of his horse in one hand, the unobliged
moon and sun of my heart's hem
in the other. It is how two unalike beings
decide to revolve, their fugitive surprising
of meaning, its semitones and rituals –
to drink rum from a tin cup near a campfire
built hastily in the woods, to think nothing
of comfort, only this splendid dread that collapses
voluptuously, that sleeps on horseback, is lashed
in the face by branches, is swift and unavailing,
is what prophecy is to disaster, words
nauseated by their shadowed outcomes.

Still, when the marksmen shot them from the saddle
didn't they fall like volunteers
of their own impetuous, wronged direction?
Didn't they find them throat on throat?

Black Pearl

As if lovemaking starts with the admission:
'Alone, I could never do it –' how
we have needed those beds wherein
we were agreeably defiled. 'Yes, it does
one good.' And only afterwards
is rather sad.

Yet we slept there and woke and took
the hands of children in our dreams,
were purified by the deadened mistake
of comparison, the way too much sunshine
makes one hunger for gray or any opposite
that asks to be taken for its seriousness,
its sensuousness of being opposite.

I am even thankful for those watered-down lives
because they seem to invest in the future
so ardently there is nothing one
can do with them but grant them serenity
like a winter sky that holds over a city
without knowing what is best for tourism.

Why did he make her feet bare
and kiss there as if it were a doing-nothing?
Where had he learned to hear best in
what pallid classroom by sitting as far as possible
from the composure of the lesson?

Was the room more quiet
when her feet were bare?
It was like asking if darkness and darkness
is still a conversation.
To love that happiness which isn't a reply
he made her feet bare, and unalone.

So to kiss them was unavoidable, an unavoidable
happiness to which neither of them contributed.
But which had still somehow to be accepted
without elevating simple good fortune.

The importance afterwards of her casual
walking away, which bore another, more gently.

Sugarcane

Some nights go on in an afterwards so secure
they don't need us, though sometimes one exactly
corresponds to its own powers of elemental tirelessness,
and a prodigious heaviness comes over it that upswings it
into taking us, like the seizure knowing is,
back into its mouth. One blue-violet night in Hawaii during
the Vietnam War pinions me against

the war's prolonged foreboding as I relive it yet
in that preposterous homecoming the generals arranged
for their men on R & R in that meant-to-be paradise. Wives
flown in to bungalows and beach-side hotels, their suitcases
crammed with department store negligees for conjugal trysts
that seem pornographic now in their psycho-erotic
rejuvenation of the killing. But he

was my husband. And I was glad he hadn't gone down
in a craze of flak in some widow-maker out of Da Nang
zigzagging over to Cambodia to drop its load. Glad
my government had a positive view of sexual continuity,
wanted its men in loving arms at their war's halftime.
We would meet, as some would not. Seven months gone –
daily letters, tapes and that telepathic hotline reserved
for saints and gods, except when women's wartime
solicitations to their mates usurped all tidy elevations.
But what did

those heavenly bodies, those angel currents make of so much
heavy panting and suppositional boudoir?
Or of the homeward-yanking fantasies' interspersals
with napalm, sniper fire, firebombing, mines – the dead,
the wounded lifted out by helicopter?
I would see you in and out of khaki
again. Was early to the island, tanning a luxurious khaki
into my sallow in a luminescent bikini after months
working the dawn shift on a medical ward.
But the night is tired of its history
and doesn't know how we got here. Children

are what it wants. Though we didn't know it, no amount of
innocent gladness of the young to meet again on earth
would bring them back. Nor could they be revived
in the glower of long rain-shattered afternoons as we labored
to push ourselves back into each other.
They were gone from us, those children.
As if disenfranchisements like this were some mercurial,
unvoiceable by-product of the country's mania, its payment
in kind for those flaming children

we took into the elsewhere. There was so much to spare you
I had to overuse loving as a balm, a cauterizing
forgetfulness to prise you to me. Maybe the exuberance
of our stretching all the way to first-love, that *always*
to each other, allowed our lack its comfortless posture,
and we were given respite in which a quiet light
thought us human enough to slough off its breath-saddened
anguish. And then I saw you

made new again in moonlight. Not as yourself, but as
more entirely made of pain in its power
of always usurping what might also
be true. As I was true in moonlight, preparing to meet you,
lifted by the raw gaiety of my brother's shipmates taking shore
leave the night before you touched down, the gleeful carload of us
emptied into a field because I'd never tasted sugarcane.
Breaking off the chalky stalks,

my juiceless sucking and licking the woody fiber
in darkness, the flat way it discarded me, as if another, greedier
mouth had been there first. Then the young man's voice,
my hand with his around it lifted, so he tore with his biting
the stalk I held, squeezing my hand until the full pressure
of his jaw passed into me
as what was needed for sweetness to yield.

And since sweet pressure is all I gave – that boy's
unguarded kiss in moonlight was yours, was any god's peephole
back to where we'd meant our love to close us,
close, in a little rest, allowing
that sweet scythe of unfoulable kindred tenderness, before

the rest. That biting down on us.
The heavy pressure that demands its sweetness as it mouths
and sucks, until it finds us with its love-letting teeth.

Kiss Without a Body

You think I don't know life
humbles us to its measure?
How the magnet of beauty tears
at the skeleton, aging it
from the inside out?
Rest here a few moments, in this body
without a body that
is love, was love. These poems will
convince more than one other
you were loved greatly
and should be again. Will it be
the way a fallen star
tells the ground about the night sky?
Will she look up? that woman
in our future? But now the book
has fallen to the floor and we
have turned to each other
on the wordless stairway
of some unlived moment where poetry
means nothing, though it is all there is
of what the night would cry
if it had two voices, this one
and the one that would answer
if it could.

White Kiss

He loves like a married man
with his cache of family treasure
securing his loan, but is singular
and cannot belong. All morning
her tigers have been busy licking
each other's stripes. Balefully
they stare up at him, this meal
in reserve, replicated at the center
of their golden eyes. But the white kiss
is merciful, senses he is inconsolable, as she is,
some orphanhood they are tending.

He sucks power from her fingertips
the way a child pushes its whole face
into the too-high fountain.
The whiteness of the kiss, like the whiteness
of ball gowns in black and white movies
swirls through time and space
and twines around them, two fated radiances
incapable of reversing the dream-cloud
flown into them by an astonishment
of migratory virgin-moments.

Her costume and rituals are set.
She ministers to his ministering, and so undoes
his unintended conquering. She wears
the widow's veil, is forbidden
to lift it or to let him lift it.
She doesn't believe the word 'forbidden'.
By whom could she be forbidden?
By whiteness itself? By the tigerness
of whiteness which adopts the flaw
of the veil in order to recirculate
its most penetrating glance.

Their kissing is an after-dark,
a firefly catching party, full of lanterns
and insect telepathy against
the palms. The darker the man
the more the moon of the kiss whitens
its one resolve, the more the fountain splashes
the open eyes of the child, the more the veil
becomes a web in which the face's faceness
forces it outside its imperial identity.

At last they are able to meet
inside the white kiss where the spider's
tender silk has crosshatched their lips
with the musky taste of the never-before
as it enters the never-again.

    The golden eyes of the tigers.
    The golden tails of the tigers.
    The switching of their golden tails.

Your Hands, Which I Love to Kiss

He laughed and took me by the wrists,
turned me until I looked him in the eyes.
'I lie to her, I lie to you, I lie
to everyone,' he said, and my paleness
was like a slap to the cheek
in the midst of applause.
He did not see my green gaze quiver.
So, without realizing, he searched out in me
the wolf to his wolf.

Our faithless clashing like glacier water then
to the stolen afternoon, those sideways kisses
that are snares to keep passion less sure
so it worries the rib cage over days
and distance. If we are to be known at all
it is by no such unfevered, calculable thing
as truth, but by those betrayals
even of illicit happiness. And now

I kiss your hands instead of your lips,
your hands which I love to kiss
because they live beyond treachery
like a child's hands pressed together
in prayer, out-knowing the words meant
for a little while to hold the eyes closed
inside belief that must begin
as a feigned immensity.

I kiss the child in you for whom the lie
is the instinctive shield against all claims.
I kiss the child in the man
to wake the man before the confession
love makes of us can be received
by any lonely, sleeping god. I kiss
the god in you, the lie, you would say,
by which I entered.

Say what you like, it's the god
who kisses, the god walking with its gleaming bucket
full of little frightened trout, the god by which
I look into your eyes,
by which my green gaze quivers
and I am unafraid.

Better Than Chance

The kiss scored better than chance when it came
to guessing liars in those lively tournaments
arranged by the Human Interest Laboratory
in San Francisco. She squared off against police officers
and judges whose low opinions spared not
any. They believed everyone
was lying all the time. The kiss watched

the mouths of potential liars, with a mind
discreet behind dark glasses. She had a knack
for spotting the variegated twitch or
double-sided spangles some lies give off
the instant they try to interweave themselves
with the truth by rushing the voice into
a quicksilver blending of quiet dawns with
coppery facades. Often a yellow, elastic light
appeared above the head of the liar, and they

would reach up with their eyes, as if choosing
an especially plump and tender lie
to pluck. She tried not to depend too much on their voices.
A liar's voice was like patent leather, a slick
son of a bitch, the phrase she liked to apply personally
to the liars once she'd found them out, walking up
with a little curtsy, and with her face
dead as a frying pan, then opening her reddest lips
the requisite slit. She was effective,

in demand. She'd honed her skills dealing blackjack
in Reno, could take in the anthill of a room and gauge
which players were about to walk across the backs of
their comrades to snap down an ace.
She was better than chance. She scored more than
80 percent, beating out psychiatrists who believed
sloppily that truth was a factor of attrition, of lies eroding
over time, or that lying was truth's prelude,
a kind of delicate foreplay. But what about

that twenty percent she'd guessed wrong?
The ones who could watch delicate skin surgery,
and deny they'd witnessed anything traumatic. Such a liar
could float junk bonds down the Mississippi, push gangsters
into cement mixers with impunity. They could start churches
called The Divine Noses of Escobar with cocaine cartels in Colombia
When they prayed on TV even God would wish

he had a nose to whoof something up. The kiss was rueful.
A lot of cheating, pilfering, stealing, murdering, manhandling,
scummy entrepreneurial, sneaky resourcefulness
was obviously going to slip by her. She puckered up and
applied herself to these hard cases. She was crazy
for them, the way the FBI was crazy for communists back
in 1955. She fantasised her own federally-funded
Core of Liars for a More Truthful America.
They would visit high schools, appear on late night TV talk shows.
But when she looked into their honest-to-God eyes, and they

told her if they gave her flowers they would just
wilt, she was that beautiful, she fell for them even more.
She was just a very silly old kiss with a passion for liars and
the lies of liars, those little darlings the truth has to lie down with
every day, summoning a will to transcendence, intimacy,
discrimination – but staying a little flexible
in case some liar should inadvertently invent the paradox
that would enliven her, the way a kiss
when it is stolen knows something you can
never find out any other way.

Like the Sigh of Women's Hair

The horse stands under my window
but its rider is gone.
I know it's a vision. I know if
I went down to it and took it
by the mane, the breath it would blow
damp into my hair, breath sweet
as any man's who came to my door
with lovemaking on his mind,
would be muffled in dream.

How like the sigh of women's hair
as it falls to the floor in a glassy slicing,
his breath over me in the morning air.
All my windows were open,
the red winter grass high to his stirrup.
When he bent to me
I could hear the saddle creak, the horse
shifting under his thighs.

The grass, the wet grass across
my ankles when he pulled me
astride. 'I'll tell you something
you won't forget in twenty years,' he said,
like the last words before sleep.
'Tell me,' I said.
But he didn't say more.
He wouldn't say more.
The horse took us down to the sea
and he wouldn't say more.

Cameo

From her sly chariot drawn by cats
she has kept one as a moon
to her vermilioned eaves. She soars
in the checkered room, pulled along
by hair that rays out astonished
like the spiritual side of a tantrum,
or the mind's casual anatomy to either side
of a sudden, sprawling daydream.

Each hour is silver, is salt
to the enfolded extract of gaiety she gives off.
Why do we envy her ravaged nest between winter
and spring if not for its tender, vacant appeal –
as if to become more sweetly dark
we had stared with her into the cave
of a cello suspended by midday's unreality,
and had seen, in the silent curvature
of its spirit's kneeling,
the workings of a velvet moan.

There Is No Daylight

like the daylight in which he makes
the clothes of me by coming near.
True, I am fierce, an ingrate to see him tangled
in his own abundance, for if he makes bait of me,
I can weave the hook so as never to be entirely also
the meal. If he thinks of me on his way to other fullness
I will be left rightly behind, as innocently
unwearied as an opened book, to be closed or
not. But if he brings me a peach or peels
an orange in my lap, I will waste daylight closer to the rose
to ask for time with him again. Though not asking

is the rule of this wild garden, and I break it most
in being roguish with his aim to pace me out,
break it the way being second to any offering
looks lovingly backward, yet won't put up with rueful fate
as a major chord. But here he is again, and I am chill
with happiness like a fearless question mark
with turquoise on its brow.
Or horses neighing before thunder.

Black Violets

If I say 'black violets' our first night
is nearly dark enough to draw this daylight rain
to memory's nomadic glistening, and I can
be there again, carrying love
to love in that room where his last heart
gave over its invisible amber. It's true,
he's evergreen in me and I make green use of him
to love you all the way back through death
into life again. I bury us in him and dig
us out again until we are a moon
that has passed through a mountain in order
to climb the night sky with no voice, no mouth,
no bodily empire except this lonely passage
for which he lends goodly silence and
the distance by which a moon can rise.

In that pang of earth you cast into me
he stepped forward, accompanied us
a little way into the present, into the sweetness
of so much yet to be lived out in this retrieval
of my unretrievable heart.
If you were two men to me there
it was to make lucid a fresh outlasting.
The one in which yours are the lips, yours
the enfolding vastness, this black rushing
of tiny fragrant faces against our skin, the violets
we feed each other petal by velvet
petal to keep the night long enough
for this new-made heart to open us in blood-darkness
into its farthest chamber.

Elegy with a Blue Pony

It is said one-third of China
is a cemetery: 'But what
a cemetery!' Henri Michaux exclaimed.
Somewhere a cemetery exists
for all the kisses I was going to
give you. Multitudes of butterflies
like to sleep there in that third
of my heart's country. Their wings
open and shut pensively, as if
the lips of the sky had come down
to announce the end of a journey,
to ruffle the meadow grass
with the azure breeze of the moment.

If, in your travels in the spirit world,
you suddenly recall those kisses you
might have had, you won't have to
live again to enjoy them.
They are waiting. You will always
be expected by my kisses.
Lie down. Let the nose
of my blue pony brush your neck.
Don't be sad I'm not with her, or
that the butterflies rise as a body
to let her pass. Don't be sad.
I'm still alive and have to follow
my kisses around. But you, you can
lie down and be enlivened, kissed
into yet another imperishable
collaboration on the way to me.

Printed in the USA
CPSIA information can be obtained
at www.ICGtesting.com
JSHW081708110424
61005JS00002B/59